EX CATHEDRA

XXVIII

PETER JOANNIDES

Copyright © 2018 by Peter Joannides
All rights reserved.

This book or any portion thereof may not be reproduced or used in any manner whatsoever without the express written permission of the publisher except for the use of brief quotations in a book review.

Printed in the United States of America

Corrected second printing, 2019

ISBN 978-1-7324338-0-9

www.PetroulisI@gmail.com

AUTHOR'S NOTE

This is the latest in the series of **Ex Cathedras** begun in 1972.

Peter Joannides

ALSO BY PETER JOANNIDES

Amán Amán!
Ex Cathedras (IX-XV)
More Ex Cathedras (XVI-XXII)
Ex Cathedra XXIII
Ex Cathedra XXIV
Ex Cathedra XXV
Ex Cathedra XXVI
Ex Cathedra XXVII

December 01, 2018

Ex Cathedra

28th Encyclical

von Herrn Doktor Professor Peter Joannides

1

One plight of writers is that, all the second printings and second editions notwithstanding, they can't really take an error or infelicitous expression back.

2

I swore there would be no more about Trump. But I can't resist this final dig.

Trump really **must** be a jerk: On top of everything else, he likes his steaks well-done.

3

Adam Gopnik and Timothy Garton Ash: two of a kind.

4

I wonder which I manage to turn off more quickly: an operatic soprano or a gaudily-costumed historical film.

5

The Windowless Monad

I'm still not disabused of philosophical solipsism.

6

So many writers often neglect the ambience of the when as they focus on the what.

7

It's fruitless to analyze dreams; just as it is to analyze poetry.

8

Highly underrated members of our technological civilization (and probably many others that I can't think of just now): plumbers, electricians, car mechanics, crane operators, welders…

9

And then there are the highly underappreciated: truck drivers, bus drivers, garbage disposers, mailmen, police officers, firemen, machine tenders…

10

Can one be opinionated and still be a determinist?

 # 10

I don't see why not, provided at least one of his opinions insists on the correctness of determinism.

(Needless to say, all of his moral judgments, no matter how vehemently held, will now have to be considered as disguised aesthetic ones.)

12

I believe that the severest extreme pain can make **anyone** cry "Uncle!"

13

We need a President who will repeal what has been repealed.

14

I've always admired and respected Queen Elizabeth of the United Kingdom.

Especially after the heartfelt declaration she made upon her father's death.

But I don't understand how she could have permitted that tasteless stunt at the London Olympics.

15

Sometimes I cry very easily.

16

It makes a difference to me knowing that someone's talk-and-behavior has been rehearsed.

17

"How full is the world of" Little Napoleons!

18

For all my rants about those who do ads, I am now, at this late date, beginning to put myself in their shoes.

19

There have been Presidents who have been ill-informed, not too bright, undeserving, prejudiced, malevolent, corrupt, even criminal…

But a laughingstock!—that is indeed unprecedented.

20

We are carried along by some sort of cause-and-effect process, and if we try to buck it, that's just another form of being carried along.

21

Those who argue against determinism are either fools or sophists.

22

I confess: I like disaster films.

23

Adam Gopnik and Steve Inskeep

I once caught a glimpse of each of these two men **whole** and on television, and found them both to be sympathetic and likeable.

It's just that the disembodied writing of the one, and the disembodied Voice of the other, seem to irritate me.

24

Reading your own work under the influence of alcohol is a beautiful experience.

25

I had a cousin, who lived in Chicago, who wouldn't eat any meal whatever without an accompanying fresh green pepper.

26

How good it is to eat good food when you're really good and hungry!

27

So much of human history has hung by a thousand threads.

28

Pre-Olympic extravaganzas and half-time capers and antics do hardly anything for me.

29

I'm beginning to think that for some, dogs and tattoos fulfill the same need.

30

I use commas when I see fit.

31

How silly of me to make sweeping pronouncements about language, literature, and poetry when I don't speak French or German or Italian or Arabic or Farsi or Chinese or Japanese or even a decent Greek.

32

Something delicious when offered in reasonable portion can never ever match its teeny-weeny sample when first encountered.

33

How in the world does a python (or a kingfisher, for that matter) ever get any enjoyment from swallowing things **whole**?

34

Oh all you computer experts: I just want to remind you that you too will be soon deleted.

John Wayne

weary, weary, weary

36

The other day I saw a documentary about money and debt. It was a cartoon type designed, presumably, to simplify things for simpletons like myself who know so little about the subject.

It started off with examples of primitive barter and went on to talk about money as a symbolic convenience and then about interest and compound interest and banking and credit and financial structures, and at about a quarter of the way through, it lost me.

There is no doubt that understanding finance-and-economics is the very least of my intellectual capacities.

The very bottom of any list.

37

I sure wish Gore Vidal were around. I'd be more than interested in what he would have to say about the current imbroglio.

38

I have the sneaking suspicion that hedge fund managers are leeches on the body politic.

39

All of a sudden there's an article in **The New Yorker** about the philosopher Peter Sloterdijk: The toast of Germany, the writer of umpteen books, the irreverent gadfly of European intellectuals…

I have never even remotely heard of him.

40

Whenever any personal prejudices seem to take hold, all I do is simply think of the children, and the prejudices evaporate instantly.

41

There is a time to do fiction, and a time not to be able to do fiction.

Ex Cathedra XXVII, # 110

It's not so much the music, it may not be at all the music; it's the lyrics.

43

In the last year or so, practically every time I sit down for lunch, that opening sentence from the **Tractatus,** "Die Welt ist alles, was der Fall ist," comes flashing before my mind.

I haven't the faintest, not the faintest, idea why.

44

I hate it when even the simplest things start not working right.

And the sad thing is I don't even have the elementary know-how to fix them.

45

Sometimes I become very aggravated when something blocks out my sun.

Sometimes I'd give anything to find a sanctuary from that merciless sun.

It's sad when I think of my innocent and youthful days.

And all because I had to grow up and learn about science and biology.

When birds are singing and chirping and tweeting, what they are, for the most part, proclaiming is:

"I'm hungry, I'm hungry, I'm hungry!"

"Wanna fuck, wanna fuck, wanna fuck!"

"Keep away, keep away, keep away from my space!"

I always made A's in math.

I memorized the rules and dutifully followed through.

But my heart wasn't really in it.

I never truly knew why or what I was doing.

To this day, when dealing with fractions, decimals, percentages, calculations, I have a hard time.

48

I love a lush green frondescence against a backdrop of crystalline and unblemished blue.

49

Newton was all obsessed with the Bible and religion. What a screwed-up and tangled contradiction!

 # 49

And, equally so, Conan Doyle and his obsession with the paranormal.

51

I still get sexually excited,

But no denouement.

52

Imagine what the world would be like if everyone were honest, and friendly, and kind, and as productive as their capabilities would allow.

53

I can't stand the phrase "his or her," and so to avoid it I will simply use "his," or resort to a circumlocution, or just violate the rules.

54

I love it when a window separates me from all those buzzing biting harm-intending inimical insects out there, and I can watch all their vain and ineffectual wormings and bumpings to get through, and revel in my god-like invulnerability.

Ex Cathedra XXVII, # 92

Too late now, but what I should have written is:

People should be polite, but writers don't have to.

56

A President who doesn't drink is no President for me.

57

Owing to many of my locutions, emphases, remarks, and perhaps heavily weighted subject matters and lists, I would like to say now, while I am still able, and for the record: I see no reason why a woman shouldn't be The Planetary Dictator.

58

I remember one day long ago, I must have been eight or nine, somewhere in upper Manhattan, seeing in big gigantic letters on a theater marquee the word "**HOY**." Of course, I had no idea what it meant, and wondered about it, but somehow that moment remains etched in my memory.

59

What you don't like to eat is probably not good for you; and what you do, probably is.

60

I wonder if all those different medicines given to me over all these many years have messed up my body in some measure?

I will try to relate a humorous story that my mother used to tell. Whether I can translate from the Anatolian Greek successfully, I don't know, but I will give it my best.

One day The King of the realm was traveling with his entourage through the countryside when he came upon some peasants about to have lunch. The peasants were preparing their repast in their hurly-burly ways when The King noticed a young man attending to his preparations with meticulous and delicate attention, including providing a tablecloth for himself as well as a number of other amenities. The King was intrigued and curious and called the young man to his side and asked him, "What is the reason, my son, for your unusual behavior?" The young man then told The King that he was from a noble family that had fallen on hard times, and that although he now had to pursue these manual labors, he could not forget his upbringing and the manners he was taught from a young age. Then The King addressed the young man thus, "I want to ask you one question and please give me your considered answer. What is the best part of a chicken?" Whereupon the young man answered with alacrity, "Why, Your Majesty, it is of course the skin." The King then invited the young man to his palace, and gave him a responsible position, and the young man was handsomely rewarded and prospered.

(continued)

When the peasants heard of the affair, one of the wily ones among them thought of what he might do to also better his fortune, and so awaited The King's next visit.

The King once again passed through the same countryside, and the wily peasant set about mimicking the ways of his fortunate companion. The King once again was intrigued but this time suspicious, and when the wily peasant offered the same story of having fallen on hard times, The King once again asked him to answer one question, "What is the best part of a cow?" And the wily peasant answered with similar earnestness, "Why, Your Majesty, it is of course the skin."

Whereupon, The King said to the wily peasant, "Stay where you are, my son, and where you belong."

When you go from a spoken tale in one language to a written version of it in another, are you interpreting or translating?

64

I traded languages for handball, and for a long time I thought it was probably a bad trade; but I am not so sure anymore.

65

Not drinking is not a badge of honor; it is a badge of dishonor.

66

Probably, the greatest single intellectual fraud of modern times: Sigmund Freud.

67

Isn't it interesting how every so often, and for hardly any reasons, I take a distinct liking to somebody. The latest: Vicente Fox of Mexico.

68

It's nothing less than a fine art to fry scallops correctly.

69

How I love a lemon that you don't have to struggle with, one that you gently squeeze and a veritable torrent of juice comes pouring forth.

70

Another one of my mother's sayings:

"When the crazy one came upon the drunkard,

the crazy one stepped aside."

In order to understand Immanuel Kant, you have to ask yourself the following question:

What is The World like to a rock (or a cadaver)?

And the answer would seem to be: no space, no time, no pleasure or pain, no aesthetics, no moralities, no cause-and-effect, no universes, no multi-universes, no big bangs, no expanding galaxies, no black holes, no dark matters, no electrons, no protons, no boson particles, no photons, no neutrinos, no quarks, no string theories…

72

There must be something to the German language that draws me to it.

73

What a charade! Reporters asking questions of the lackey presidential press secretary (of all parties) when they already know the answers they're going to get.

74

I don't remember people very often using the words "iconic" and "kudos" in the old days; and as for the phrase "goes viral," not at all.

In any case, all three are not much to my liking.

75

How neglected is Protagoras, probably the greatest of the Ancients.

76

In all the turmoil of the present-day Middle East, invariably all sorts of maps and more maps are displayed, and they, more often than not, include Cyprus.

And every time I see Cyprus and that long thin peninsula jutting into the northeast, I think of Frank's hometown of Rizokarpaso (and the episode of my wallet plopping down the outhouse hole into the waiting pit below).

77

The Jumble (puzzle) has taught me a good many things: strategy, experimentation, tactics, reassessments, solutions.

Current Events (April 13, 2018)

I never realized that the term "slimeball" could have such a boomerang effect.

79

Even the most infinitesimal spot on my shirt or trousers will drive me crazy until I get rid of it.

I'd love to send this questionnaire to all those who remember:

Who was better at accents and imitations—Peter Sellers or Sid Caesar?

81

I could forgive a Vegan (although not an easy thing to do), but a teetotaler—**NO!**

82

My **2nd** most favored Shakespearian line:

"It is a tale told by an idiot, full of sound and fury, signifying nothing."

83

I'd be more than happy if we could create equivalent filet mignons without killing animals.

84

I wonder if, sometime in the future, some professor will be giving a whole semester's seminar on "**Amán Amán! plus**"?

85

When it comes to The Aliens, I don't rule anything out.

86

I wish I weren't so "advanced" (with "Modern Marvels" and all that), so that I could muster the patience and fortitude to read **Madame Bovary**.

87

I'm an expert on changing my mind.

The only **real** Jane in the Tarzan movies was Maureen O'Sullivan.

89

Any animal as intelligent as Man is bound to be curious about, manipulative of, experimental with, and interpersonally involved by, his genitalia, and the more intelligent, the more pronounced his interest.

It's a wonder that such an obvious dictum hasn't been more often expressed as directly as I have just done.

90

Sometimes it's just the icing on the cake. The rest of it might as well be thrown away.

It seems that family is the one true and binding unit.

There may be friendship that could match it, but (especially in this day and age) that is something that is few and far between.

92

I'm like a dog that sniffs; don't ask me for intellectual justifications.

93

The News is getting more and more uninteresting every day.

94

Nothing quite as off-putting as writers who take such great pains to show how clever and learned they are.

95

I can't believe some of the glib and not unintelligent apologists for, and defenders of, the current administration in the op-ed pages of **The Wall Street Journal**.

What matter of happenstance can make such twisted and convoluted casuists come creeping out of the woodwork?

96

How entrancing it was to hear the News one day from a lady with a West Indian accent in Belize.

97

"Deplorables" was exactly right.

Even though humankind may be the fodder and fertilizer for the mechano-electronico beings that may come and supplant, still, despite all the pain and suffering, the bloodless things will never know what they missed.

99

What crushes me more than anything else are handicapped children.

100

Accidents happen in a flash.

101

With so many thinkers, their tomes could be reduced to a few well-written pages.

102

What is this rap? It has no connection with authentic African music or even Caribbean whatsoever.

Just an American musical bastardy.

103

A long way after Nero Wolfe and Sherlock Holmes is The Saint. And a long way after The Saint is Mike Hammer.

Why is it that a movie version of anything actual or imaginatively written almost invariably falls on its face.

Or is, occasionally, a success simply on its own merits, and hardly related to its supposed antecedent.

105

A pardon for Blagojevich will be the straw that broke the camel's back.

My back.

106

I suspect that all countries, large **and small**, have the **richness** that has Greece.

I'm so sorry I can't partake of each and every one.

Atrocities throughout History.

Benevolence throughout History.

108

I would like to see the current President of the United States slowly and politely escorted off the White House grounds.

109

I once said I would love to experience a monsoon, 40 days and 40 nights of pounding, unremitting rain.

That was, clearly, an exaggeration.

But, even so, there is something about a **heavy** rain that attracts.

110

It was many years ago, so many many years ago; and now, once again, in my old age: Pine Bros. Honey Cough Drops.

111

I've always thought of Jacksonville as somehow incidental. It never had much to do with my plans, goals, travels, desires, imaginations…

And now I've suddenly realized I have spent most of my life in Jacksonville.

112

Who in hell would be a Vegan, and also a teetotaler?

I know, a fiery and eloquent orator, a Democrat, and a Contender.

I once found a wallet somewhere on the turf at Jacksonville Beach. I kept the 30 or 40 dollars (I don't remember the exact amount) and turned the wallet in with its papers and identifications to the nearest police station.

Another of my sins, which should have been mentioned in my Confessional Section (**peccata venialia**) along with stealing towels from the Y, and scurrying off when the cashier gave me the wrong change in my favor, as well as registering for classes at JU under the GI Bill without ever attending. (Ninetta's badgering.)

I'm sure I would have mentioned this had I remembered it.

114

There's something about handball that's different from all other sports.

("Better than" is what I obviously have in mind.)

115

I don't know what I would have done without the help and company of my friend and neighbor, George Hiscock.

Knowing George for the last several years has been a whole new education.

116

In grammar, what is technically correct isn't always the right choice.

117

So many public officials are quite intelligent but strikingly sophistic.

(Most of the time they're usually Republicans.)

((Orrin Hatch comes quickly to mind.))

118

There's some truth (sometimes not very much) to just about any viewpoint.

119

What am I doing commenting on the political turmoils of the day when they will all be soon forgotten.

Can't help it. Caught up in the throes of the moment.

120

All Tarzans, both before and after Johnny Weissmuller, were pitiful.

121

On Sundays and holidays, it's better to stay home.

And just look at these men: their eye saith it—they know nothing better on earth than to lie with a woman.
Filth is at the bottom of their souls; and alas! if their filth hath still spirit in it!
Would that ye were perfect—at least as animals! But to animals belongeth innocence.
Do I counsel you to slay your instincts? I counsel you to innocence in your instincts.

—**Zarathustra** "Chastity"

For many years, I'm afraid, I would have had to plead somewhat guilty to this charge.

123

With quite a few doctors: the blind leading the blind.

124

For some people, "Fuck you!" is the only appropriate and final remark.

125

When a film is in a foreign setting, and the actors are supposed to be speaking a foreign language, I would prefer that they did so.

I'd rather have the subtitles, as frustrating as they are, than the phony English.

126

I don't know what unnerves me more: tattoos or graffiti.

125

For example, **The Hindenburg**.

(Of course, this would require a whole new raft of German-speaking actors.)

"But I never believed in the people when they spake of great men—and I hold to my belief that it was a reversed cripple, who had too little of everything, and too much of one thing."

—**Zarathustra** "Redemption"

How germane to the situation at hand.

129

I don't even understand many of the cartoons in **The New Yorker**, much less find them terribly funny.

But that recent one about a divided highway with on the left back-to-back traffic as far as the eye could see, and a lone car barrelling down the two empty lanes on the right, with a sign saying "Schadenfreude Next 20 Miles," really got to me.

I couldn't stop laughing for a full five minutes, and some time thereafter.

130

To this day, I have never understood the how or why or need of spitting.

It is something repugnant and utterly foreign to my nature.

Spokespersons = Puppets

132

If there'll be any historians still around in the coming tomorrows, they'll have a field day with the current President and his revolving administration.

I remember the old days when a group of Cypriots would play 5-card stud poker.

When the dealer handed out a card that had no apparent value given the showing hand, he would sometimes say **típota** (nothing) or sometimes **psakí!**

I have always wondered what **psakí!** meant. Unfortunately, there aren't many old-timers left to ask. After doing a lot of research and inquiries (including a call to the Cypriot Embassy in Washington where a polite **young** consular officer told me that in the Cypriot dialect it is spelled and pronounced **psatzí** and that it meant "poison"), I have finally settled on "poison," although I remember it pronounced **psakí**.

I'm still not satisfied, and would like to hear the answer from the lips of a card-playing old-timer, if I can find one.

This is getting ridiculous, one old-timer trying to find a still-older old-timer.

134

Narrators of documentary films should be heard and not seen.

I thought I had reviewed and exhausted all remote islands.

And now suddenly I learn of a new one that somehow escaped me: The Cocos (Keeling) islands, deep and isolated in the middle of the Indian Ocean.

I would love to visit.

But then I think of (both the benign and) the malign reaches of globalization, and I can just imagine the inanities that are bound to occur, even there.

136

A very good friend is insisting that the upcoming one-on-one Presidential summit of the Russian Federation and the United States will be between a gangster and a swindler.

137

It's really embarrassing to watch the current President confer and hobnob and give speeches with foreign leaders.

It's as if one were suddenly plucked from the streets, forced into ill-fitting dress, and instructed, with his coarse intonations, on how to mouth bromides and platitudes.

No Lackawanna 16356

One day in Chile, while staying at a lakeside hotel with a stunning view, I one of a few guests, possibly the only one, and thinking that here, in this tranquil setting with my pisco sour and pursuing the scintillating sun, the magic moment was bound to happen.

But all I remember is trying so hard to make it happen.

What happened to Yugoslavia after WWII? It must take quite an expert to know all the factions, upheavals, wars, religions, tensions, executions, massacres, minorities within without all the constituent Republics.

140

I'm beginning to think **Cast Away** should be included in the top 10 films of modern times.

My God! All the books that I haven't read (and that I guess I was supposed to):

The Great Gatsby
War and Peace
The Stranger
The Divine Comedy
One Hundred Years of Solitude
Sorrows of Young Werther
The Scarlet Letter
Catch-22
For Whom the Bell Tolls
To Kill a Mockingbird
Buddenbrooks
Lolita
Doctor Zhivago
The Bell Jar
One Day in the Life of Ivan Denisovich
The Red and the Black
Tristram Shandy
Sophie's Choice
Fathers and Sons
Rabbit is Rich
Slaughterhouse-Five
Invisible Man
and on and on and on…

Two paragraphs of legalese, including those of the Supreme Court, is about my limit before I start pining for fresh air.

143

I'm sick and tired of hearing about the President's "base."

God help and preserve us from the President's "base."

The challenge for adults is to **match** the deeds of adulthood with the wonder of childhood.

145

A speech delivered by a political ninny and written by a speechwriter.

What could be more **disingenuous** (not to use a far harsher word)?

146

I seem to have gotten myself into a routine with the morning paper: "Dennis the Menace," "The Lockhorns," "Blondie," "Marmaduke," "Beetle Bailey," and nothing and nobody else.

147

Everyone lives in a prison (except perhaps the wandering and picaresque hero). It's just that some prisons are more spacious and commodious than others.

I hardly remember my teaching experiences, not only with Maryland but also at Jacksonville as well. It's as if my mind has become a perfect blank—a kind of automatic pilot—with everything simply expunged from my memory.

What I do remember is what I did and thought and shared in my travels and with friends and lovers, as well as the pain and frustration and occasional delight of my writing, but hardly a thing about what happened in the classroom.

I don't think this means I did a bad job. I was organized, responsible, and conscientious, and I think I fulfilled my obligations (although I do remember sometimes shaving a minute or so of time off the duration of classes).

The whole thing is uncanny.

The memory of teaching seems to have just been somehow removed from my mind.

149

I've said some nasty things about painters and painting, but I think I'm now prepared to like **some** impressionist work.

150

Noam Chomsky is no doubt a progressive thinker and enlightened critic, and a man of considerable accomplishments, or so I hear,

                                      but he puts me to sleep.

151

All those millions and billions of dollars devoted to Defense and Armaments owing to national suspicions and animosities. Imagine under a responsible, strict, and benevolent Planetary Authority, how much more wisely those billions could be spent.

The Peasant Marey

Oh how many **unrecorded** kindnesses have happened in this world!

153

This is a true proposition:

Every time one pulls out of his driveway and down the street to his destination, he is affecting the driving patterns and their outcomes all over the country; and indeed the world.

As uninvolved as I am:

You cannot argue with physical predictions based upon exact mathematical calculations.

I hardly had a connection with black people as far back as I can remember. (Of course, I'm not counting Beulah and Lessie and Perla who worked for Uncle Nick at the Acropole Bakery during my early teens and the laughter and bantering that went on there these ages ago.) There was not a single black cadet at Fork Union that I remember, nor a single black student at the University of Virginia, and certainly no black individuals involved in the Philosophy Department at Cornell. In all my years with Maryland and Jacksonville University, I don't recall a single black faculty member, nor do I remember ever having a single black student. And during my handball days, not a player in Hampton or Norfolk or Jacksonville or Flamingo Park or anywhere else in Florida, until toward my waning days there was finally Walt Frazier with whom there was endless joking and challenging and kibitzing. In all my years at the Jacksonville YMCA, beginning in 1967, I don't remember a single black member until relatively recently.

Except for trips abroad where I met various black people, and especially in the Caribbean where I had the pleasure and good fortune of making a good friend, I think I have lived most of my life in the US in a white bubble.

(continued)

156

It is only in the last few years at the YMCA, I have come to know and interact with black members. (And, dare I say it, generally speaking they have been friendlier, warmer, and more simpatico than whites.)

(And I can't resist mentioning that behind the serving line at Piccadilly, the black ladies were always more generous than their white counterparts.)

157

In **White Heat** Cagney goes out not with a whimper but a Bang.

158

One individual (or even animal) in great pain invalidates all sloppy and slipshod generalizations.

The ideal family: 2 girls and 2 boys.

Next: 3 girls and 1 boy.

Next: 3 boys and 1 girl.

Next: 4 girls.

Last: 4 boys. (A tragedy.)

160

All my life I've liked shellfish over fish.

I remember, once again these ages ago, one day Cyrus and I went to the movies to see **Saboteur**. And in the scene at the end where the villain (Norman Lloyd) is barely hanging on with his hands to an upper ledge of the Statue of Liberty and Robert Cummings (the hero) is trying to save him by grabbing on to the sleeve of his jacket, Lloyd's jacket begins to slowly unravel.

And as Lloyd plummets to his death, Cyrus wisecracks in a not too soft a voice, "Aw, cheap material!"

And our neighboring movie-goers in front of us all turned around and gave us the dirtiest look.

162

I've always had some sort of mental block with the word "venue."

And now it's "app" and "algorithm."

163

Melon at its best has got it all over watermelon at its best.

"The American Experience. Where we've been. Where we are. Where we are going."

Who in hell is this "we" that seems to have some sort of collective consciousness, that lives through all change and time, and is a witness to the whole panorama? There is no such being, and a somewhat false and sentimental note is being struck here. There are only individuals: children whose life has been snuffed out before they've hardly had a chance to know anything, soldiers cut down and maimed in their prime on the battlefield, millions living a sort of humdrum and predictable existence (although each unique and different from one another), destitutes and flaunting multimillionaires, old men who can't remember what they had for breakfast in the morning...

I suppose historians should be allowed a bit of literary license, a sort of poetic indulgence, but for my part I prefer my history to be more statistical, specific, scientific, accurate, and truthful, even though it may be somewhat drier.

(The irony here is the historian who triggered this entry, as well as # **158**, is a man whom I like and respect. I suspect he was persuaded to narrate one of these otherwise excellent but trilly documentaries.)

I remember the imperiousness of sex, how achingly and screamingly hot in the groin it could get, and that one could do practically anything to assuage it.

I can identify.

People who abhor the limelight being photographed telling us how much they abhor the limelight.

167

Adjunct Professor of jazz, University of…

Why not an Adjunct Professor of poker?

Or even an Adjunct Professor of horseshoe pitching?

168

Women screaming into a microphone is not music; it's just women screaming into a microphone.

169

"The History of Technology from Earliest Times to the Present."

I can't think of a more interesting topic.

170

I miss **ylistrítha** (purslane) in my salad.

Typos that somehow manage to get through the gamut of the most extensive and collective scrutiny do nothing less than crucify me.

172

The thing is to be brave in your youth, not in your old age.

173

Believe it or not, I'm still learning my English. Not long ago, when Nona asked me, "Did you get the skinny on that?" I had no idea what she was talking about.

174

There's nothing like surgery, when it's successful.

175

Believe it or not, I've always wanted to be The Planetary Dictator, only to do some good.

In fact, I would welcome being anonymous, and to **remain** so—forever.

176

I'm sorry, all that Nashville country music does nothing for me.

177

There have been so many near-tragedies in my life, it's nothing less than a wonder that I've somehow escaped them all.

A few days ago, coming upon an artifact, an old postcard from my Uncle John to my father and mother: From "Pvt. John E. Loides 32596832 Co. H. 1229 R. C. Fort Dix, N.J. Postage Free to Service Men Dec.14 1942" to "Mr. and Mrs. Paul and Mary Joannides 10 Louis St. Lodi, N.J."

What a sudden flood and flurry of long-forgotten memories and feelings.

175

All well and good to have the power and desire to do good. But this seems to involve two important conditions:

A) You must know what it is that is good.

B) You must have some idea how to successfully bring about this good.

These are pretty daunting presuppositions.

180

I've always been in awe of batteries, and all the amazing things they do.

181

Which is the supreme dessert: crème caramel or muhallebi?

They're all gone: Cyrus is gone, Bob Bryan (a man of once sterling character and intellect) might as well be gone, Walter Bass is gone, Harriet is gone, Nick Cassas is gone, Eli Bassett is gone, Jim and Nancy are gone, Dave Scales is gone, Mihalis Lapatsis is gone, neighbor Dick Kennedy is gone, old Costa is gone, Costa Achillopulo is gone, Pat Delapenha is gone, Sam Moss is probably gone, Alex Panas is gone, Ranji Chandisingh is gone, Paula is close to being gone...

Who's left? Cary Karageorge, Rogelio Francisco Anduaga de Arias (who will probably outlive us all, his forebears hailing from the Amazon rain forest), Charlie Ruhlin, Connie(?), Yours truly, cousin Vasso, Geraldine Bryan, Chuck Moore (although not a fair inclusion, being considerably younger), David Smith (ditto)...

I wonder who will be the Last of the Mohicans?

183

By rights, Vegans should only eat fruit.

Maybe we should coin a new word: "Fruitans."

184

I'm trying hard not to repeat myself.

I don't know who that screwball modern singer is who is jazzing up the old tune **It Had to Be You** with all the over-screaming and emphases in the wrong places and a tempo expressly tailored for lunkheads.

What a travesty of a beautiful old song.

(This can be said for quite a few modern renditions ((distortions)) of beautiful old songs.)

186

Just as I am about to get over my problem with Southerners, up pops a mouthy senatorial Southerner to reinforce it.

187

The President is proud of never having had a beer.

This should be enough to disqualify him for the office.

188

I follow no set rule about how many spaces should succeed a colon. Sometimes it's one, sometimes two, depending upon the look of the writing.

189

Senator Mitch McConnell: The Ghoul.

190

I keep forgetting that people were once young, and very young, and very very young.

The long road to understanding and to sainthood.

Some of the "poems" in **The New Yorker** are just plain nonsense—a sort of pretentious plain nonsense.

You shouldn't have to be a super-cryptologist to fathom a poem.

192

Now, I'm not forgetting that people, unless they've been cut down prematurely, get old, and very old, and very very old.

The long road to understanding and to sainthood.

193

In a finer world, when inhabitants fleeing from a devastating hurricane knock on your door, you unhesitatingly take them in.

Pat Buchanan: Is that long passed-by clown still around?

195

The best and only redeeming thing about a lot of otherwise terrible films is just the technology depicted.

I am not unaware that, although my attention is largely skewed to my country The United States, there may be writers, comedians, statesmen, actors, intellectuals, moral leaders… in many another land, and even a small land, that may be the equals, if not the betters, of my own.

I've finally decided: my favorite of the syndicated cartoons is "The Lockhorns."

198

What Maya is able to do with her smart phone absolutely electrifies my mind.

I think I'm being left far behind.

199

I stand in wonder at the laws of physics: how exact they are, and that you violate them at your peril.

(Biological and physiological thresholds are subclasses of these laws.)

200

The age-old enemy is pain: physical pain, psychological pain, self-conjured pain.

201

I never could understand the inordinate interest some have in who their ancestors were.